The Mallaig Railway

ISBN 978-0-905489-89-6

The Mallaig Railway

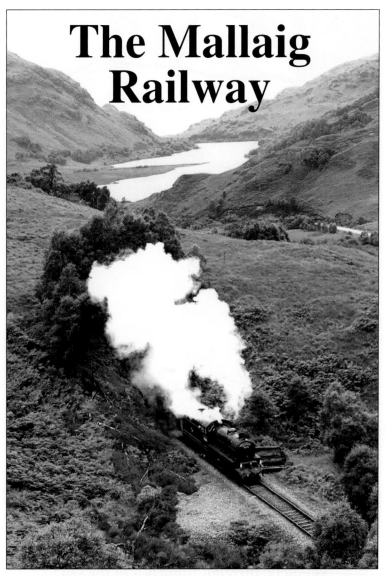

**A contemporary guide to the line reprinted with colour
illustrations celebrating the return of steam**

Northern Books
from Famedram

Through woods, beside lochs, across rivers, over viaducts, through tunnels – to the sea. The incomparable Mallaig Railway.

The Race to the Atlantic

DRIVING a railway from the heartlands of Scotland to the shores of the Atlantic had been a dream that pre-occupied the railway fanatics of the late 19th century. Reaching Fort William, which the West Highland did in 1894, did not satisfy the craving and no sooner had the cheering died away in 'The Garrison' than the push was on to continue to the *real* ocean.

Oban had finally been reached (after a monumental struggle) by the Callander & Oban Railway in 1880, but the prize of heavy fish traffic still beckoned and the race was on from Dingwall in the north and Fort William farther south to bag it. Happily this was a time when economic caution did not play too large a part in the calculation of priorities; if it had then the railway map of Scotland would have shown far, far fewer thin, meandering lines.

There were some inspired landowners in those times, too (along with some difficult ones), and money could be squeezed out of a Goverment not totally deaf to the needs of the less favoured areas. So it was that the finance was finally gathered together to push on from Fort William all the way to Mallaig. Thanks to some innovative building techniques using the still fairly revolutionary material concrete, the battle to drive through glens, under mountains and over rivers was won and on April 1, 1901 the sound of steam was heard in Mallaig.

The years that followed, though they never produced the passenger returns once hoped for, certainly bore witness to plenty of activity at the fish quays and special after special departed for destinations far to the south at all hours of the night and day.

But this golden (or silver) age was to end and the axe brandished by the late Dr Beeching loomed ominously over the line. Thanks to solid support from the local community the line was spared from closure during the 60s and through the 70s glimmers of hope appeared in the upsurge of summer use by visitors from all over the world.

Eventually this trend got the recognition it deserved and the inspired decision was taken to run steam excursions over the whole 40 mile journey. It proved a huge success. Hence the re-printing (with new illustrations) of this original guide.

Fort William to Mallaig

THE NEW LINE, the first sod of which was cut by Lady Margaret Cameron of Locheil, in January 1897, took four years to construct, and was opened to traffic on April 1, 1901. The work was of a difficult and troublesome nature, there being a preponderance of heavy rock cuttings, while much ingenuity had to be exercised in the formation of certain parts of the track owing to the peaty nature of the soil. The cost of the forty miles of single track between Banavie and Mallaig is estimated at nearly £540,000, or about £13,000 per mile.

Leaving Fort William, passing the Nevis Distillery, and crossing the Nevis, the line branches off to the left, and skirts the shores of Loch Linnhe. Stretching away to the west as far as the eye can reach are the blue waters of Loch Linnhe, nestling at the foot of the wooded and heather-clad hills of Lochaber and Ardgour, and presenting a scene of beauty characteristically Highland.

To the right, by the banks of the Lochy, a little above where it enters Loch Linnhe, will be observed the picturesque ruins of old Inverlochy Castle, a stronghold of the Comyn family, dating at least from the time of Edward I, but on whose site, tradition says, once existed an ancient city and castle where the Pictish kings resided at intervals,

Into open country after crossing the Nevis

and where King Achaius, in 790 A.D. signed a treaty with Charlemagne. The neighbourhood was the scene of at least two important battles.

In 1431 Donald Balloch, cousin-german of Ross, with his Islesmen, aided by the Lochaber clans, defeated the forces of James I, and on Sunday, February 2, 1645, the Royalist forces under the Marquis of Montrose, completely routed the army 'for the Covenant,' under the Marquis of Argyle. Scott weaves the story with graphic detail on to his *Legend of Montrose,* and narrates it fascinatingly in his *Tales of a Grandfather.*

Crossing the Lochy and Corpach Moss we reach Banavie. Close at hand will be found the spacious and comfortable Banavie Hotel which looks towards Ben Nevis, and commands on fine days a magnificent view of the monarch of

Maude *on the swing bridge over the Caledonian Canal at Banavie*
British mountains.

Just beyond the station the line is carried across the
Caledonian Canal on a swing bridge of 50 feet span, and
traverses crofting lands for a little over a mile until Corpach
is reached. Here steamers, which sail daily during the season

to Inverness, pass from Loch Linnhe into the Caledonian Canal through a remarkable series of eight locks known as 'Neptune's Staircase.'

A little beyond Corpach we pass on the right, Kilmallie Parish Church. The obelisk in the churchyard was erected in memory of Col. John Cameron of Fassiefearn, who fell at Quatre Bras in command of the 92nd Highlanders, on July 16, 1815.

The epitaph on the monument was written by Sir Walter Scott, who, in his Waterloo, refers in touching terms to Cameron's death. There is also, near the obelisk, an Ionic cross in memory of Mary Mackellar, the Gaelic poetess and in front of the church is a monument in memory of General Sir Alexander Cameron, K.C.B., K.C.H., of Inveraliot, a distinguished officer of the Peninsular War.

The line now runs quite close to the shores of Loch Eil, which after we pass the narrows of Annat widens out and forms a picturesque sheet of water. An excellent view of the country is obtained as the train steams along the shores of the loch. On the west will be seen the Sgur (i.e. a sharp rock) Donald, from which stretches backwards towards Ben Nevis, a range of beautiful hills, nicely wooded in parts, while at their base lie the green fields and cottages of Lord Morton's crofters.

On the right of the line will be seen the shooting lodge of Achadalieu, which occupies a site of great natural beauty and privacy. It was on the shores of Loch Eil that the memorable fight took place between Sir Ewen Cameron of Loeheil and an officer from General Monk's garrison, and which ended in Locheil planting his teeth in the officer's throat and biting a piece clean out. The incident suggested to Sir Walter Scott the combat between Fitz James and Roderick Dhu, which he has immortalized in *The Lady of the Lake.*

Proceeding, we pass, on the right. Fassiefearn (or Fassfern) House, the birthplace of Col. John Cameron of Quatre Bras fame. Prince Charlie slept here on August 23, 1745, four nights after the Royal Standard was raised at Glenfinnan.

About a mile further on is Corriebeg where, tradition says, one of the last wolves seen in this part of the country was killed. At the head of the loch we reach Locheilside.

The district, known as Kinlocheil, is also associated with the memory of Prince Charlie. Here the news that Sir John Cope was marching by Dalwhinnie to Fort Augustus reached him. He also encamped here on the night of August 22, 1745; and hence he issued his retaliatory proclamation, offering for the capture of the 'usurper King George' the sum of £30 – afterwards altered to £30,000 – which was the

Corpach station

price set by the government of the day on his own head.

Crossing the Fionne Lighe River (the White Stream) by a double span bridge we pass on the left Drumasallie – the salting bridge.

At this spot in the days when Loch Eil was a celebrated fishing ground large quantities of fish were prepared and salted, and shipped to France and Spain. To the right is the glen known as Fionnlighe, through which runs the river of that name.

The flat strath that stretches from Loch Eil to Loch Shiel is now entered upon, and with the Dubh Lighe River (the Black Stream) on our left and great mountains rising on either side the scene is a most delightful and impressive one.

Crossing the Dubh Lighe and the public road, Craigaig, a shooting lodge of the Earl of Morton's, is passed on the left, a glimpse is also got on the left of the Callop River, which flows from Glen Duiblighe in to Loch Shiel.

From this point the line ascends a steep gradient – 1 in 45 – from the summit of which we obtain a glimpse of Glenaladale House, the old family residence of a branch of the MacDonalds, Glen Callop, and Loch Shiel. Another run through a deep cutting brings us in sight of far-famed Glen-finnan and the mighty viaduct which carries the line over the river and the valley.

This structure, one of the engineering triumphs of the line, is 1248 feet in length and 100 feet high. It has 21 spans of 50 feet each, and it is built wholly of concrete, made of cement and crushed rock quarried from deep cuttings through which the line passes at either end of the viaduct.

From the viaduct is seen the flat ground at the head of Loch Shiel and the round tower surmounted by the Highland figure known as 'Prince Charlie's Monument.'

It marks the spot where the Jacobite standard was un-

Maude *makes her historic crossing of the Glenfinnan viaduct – this unique shot is also available as a poster and as a postcard.*

furled by the Marquis of Tulliebardine, an ancestor of the present Duke of Athole, and where Prince Charlie was joined by Locheil and the other Highland chiefs who shared his fortunes, or rather misfortunes till the last ray of hope died on the fatal field of Culloden. The monument was erected by the late Alexander MacDonald of Glenaladale, and a tablet on it records the transaction in Latin, Gaelic, and English.

The English inscription runs:

"On the spot where Prince Charles Edward first raised his standard, on the 19th day of August, 1745, when he made the daring and romantic attempt to recover a throne lost by the imprudence of his ancestors, this column was erected by Alexander MacDonald, Esq., of Glenaladale, to commemorate the generous zeal, the undaunted bravery, and the inviolable fidelity of his forefathers and the rest of those who fought and bled in

that unfortunate enterprise.

This pillar is now, alas! also become the monument of its amiable and accomplished founder, who before it was finished, died in Edinburgh on 4th day of January, 1815, at the early age of twenty-eight years."

The scenery of the Loch Shiel is very grand and wild. In his wanderings here Prince Charlie on one occasion broke through a cordon of his foes in a manner at once bold and ingenious. His attendants cut down and hollowed out a tree in which the Prince was laid. They then swam across the lake dragging after them the extemporised boat with its precious freight.

To avoid exciting suspicion the boat was sunk on the further side, and years after it was recovered in a good state of preservation.

Glenfinnan Station is reached shortly after crossing the viaduct, and for a considerable time scenes of aspiring majesty and grandeur continue to meet our astonished gaze. Beyond Glenfinnan the line continues to rise and takes a rather sharp curve behind the Stagehouse Inn.

It is perhaps worthy of mention that the road from here to Arisaig, a distance of 20 miles, was made by Telford in the beginning of the last century. The cost, which was between £16,000 and £18,000, was borne by Clanranald, whose country we are now passing through.

Passing through two tunnels and crossing a winding narrow valley by two viaducts in quick succession we reach the summit, 394 feet. The line again rapidly descends and a short run brings us to Loch Eilt, a beautiful sheet of water, studded with islets clad with pines of deepest green, and with hills towering on either side.

Just beyond the head of Loch Eilt, at Arieniskill, the

Overleaf: panoramic views over the Sound of Sleat to Skye from Kinloid

Glenfinnan station plays host to the film-makers

River Ailort is crossed. The line now runs alongside the public road, to the left, and between this point and Lochailort Station there will be observed a monument to the late Mr MacCallum of Kinlochailort Hotel.

Emerging from a tunnel – the third on the line – the wild

Lochailort station: sadly reduced to a bus shelter in the Sprinter era

and rugged scenery of Lochailort – or Kinlochailort – is seen to advantage from the train.

In front lie the beautiful waters of the loch, studded with islands, to the left is seen amid trees in the deep shadows of the mountains of Moidart, Inverailort, the residence of Mrs Head, grand-daughter of General Sir Alexander Cameron, already referred to; beyond this rises Fros Bheinn, 2876 feet, while a picturesque background is formed by the distant hills of Ardnamurchan.

Leaving Loch Ailort the line crosses the narrow, mountainous peninsula of Ardnish which separates Loch Ailort from Loch-nan Uamh. Immediately beyond the station we enter a tunnel, emerging from which we see on the left the Roman Catholic Chapel. Further on the line, curving in a south westerly direction, is carried over a shallow part of Loch Dubh on a pitched slope embankment.

We now cross the Arnabol Burn by a concrete viaduct of

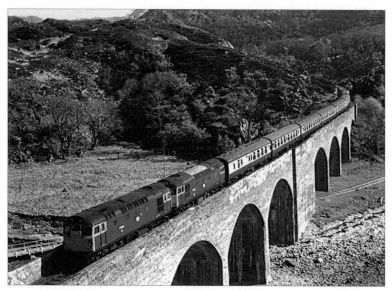

Double diesel power hauls a long excursion train over Glen Mamrie

six spans, each 50 feet. The water, and especially after heavy
rains, as it rushes seawards over a rocky and boulder strewn
bed presents a fine sight. A little further on Glen Mamrie
is crossed by a viaduct of eight spans of 50 feet each. At
this point we obtain a magnificent view of Loch-nan-Uamh
(Loch of the Caves) with its rock-bound shores and ever
changing green waters.

Far out in the ocean stands Sgurr of Eigg, with the island
of Muck on its left, and the mountains of Rum on its right.

The extraordinary beauty of this scene is further en-
hanced by the fresh, clear, and ozone-laden breezes blown
in from the Atlantic, bringing new zest to the mind and body
of the traveller. Stretching away to the right is Glen Mamrie,
but its beauty is overshadowed by the manifold attractions to
be seen seawards.

Loeh-nan-Uamh is a memorable spot, and it was here
that the French frigate Doutelle anchored on July 25, 1745,

Snow on the hills for an early spring excursion to Mallaig

with Prince Charlie on board. Here he received the chiefs and leading gentry of the surrounding country, and discussed plans for rising.

The history of the '45 has nothing more interesting than the narration of how the Prince paced the quarter-deck with MacDonald of Borrodale on the evening after his arrival, and talked the young chieftain over to embark in the luckless enterprise.

Beyond the viaduct, we pass through four tunnels, 150 feet, 270 feet and 195 feet and 490 feet, respectively, in quick succession, cross Glen Beasdale by a long embankment, and then through one of the deepest cuttings (60 feet) on the line, reaching Beasdale, the private station for Arisaig House.

At Borrodale we encounter the longest tunnel on the route. Its length is 1050 feet, and as we emerge from it we get a capital view of Arisaig House to the left. In another

second we are crossing the Borrodale Burn by an ornamen-
tal concrete viaduct of three spans, two of 20 feet and one of
127 feet 6 inches. This structure is believed to possess the
largest concrete span of any bridge yet made.

Arisaig House, the residence of Mrs. Nicholson, was

built by the late Mr. Astley, the American millionare. It is
situated on the rising ground on the opposite side of the
valley amidst lovely grounds and shadowy woods, and from
its position commands an extensive view of the surrounding

country.

This is the district known as Borrodale, inseparably associated with the final wanderings of Prince Charlie and his escape to France on September 20, 1746.

"On hills that are by richt his ain,
He roves a lonely stranger,
On ev'ry side he's pressed by want,
On ev'ry side is danger:
Yestreen I met him in a Glen,
My heart maist burstit fairly,
For sadly changed indeed was he,
Oh, wae's me for Prince Charlie!"

The fertile valley lying deep down to the left, with Loch-nan Uamh beyond, and Eigg in the distance combine in forming a picture upon which the artistic eye will love to

A derelict Beasdale station pre restoration as a private dwelling house

dwell. Proceeding across a low-lying moss and crossing the Brunery Burn, Arisaig Station is soon reached.

Here Loch-na-Cilltean, with the numerous islands which surround its mouth, is seen to full advantage, in addition to the features we have just seen mentioned. The wooded strath of Arisaig is also seen through the trees on our left.

Beyond Arisaig we pass through two cuttings, and then encounter a series of panoramic views which no amount of cold ink could ever convey to the reader one tenth part of their glory. A wide sweep of water, ranges of hills, and islands of all shapes and sizes dominate the major portion of the picture, while the foreground is prettily filled in with many bays radiant with the loveliest white sand.

For the next four or five miles our course lies through the Arisaig peat moss, Mointeach Mhor, on the borders of which are numerous crofts.

Approaching the Beasdale bank

On our left is the rock-bound coast of Morar, on the right the hills of South Morar. As we proceed a view of Loch Morar may be had to the right, but it is best seen when we

Evening sun and steam at Arisaig station

cross Morar River by the substantial four-span viaduct.

Loch Morar, contains salmon, sea trout, and loch trout in great abundance.

The Morar is only three quarters of a mile in length, but the scenery along its banks is strikingly picturesque, and in its short course it can boast of three waterfalls. As the train

Steam vs. diesel at Mallaig, as the Jacobite leaves the Sprinter standing

crosses the viaduct the rushing, noisy stream, on which are many anglers plying 'the gentle art' – for the Morar yields capital sport – forms an animated, and an exciting scene.

From Morar station the line passes through a valley and emerges on the Sound of Sleat at Glasnacardoch, from whence it is carried through alternate cutting and short embankment to its termination at Mallaig.

Here new and commodious hotels have been erected, and the tourist or sportsman will find his requirements catered for in an admirable manner by a management of wide experience in the business.

A few yards beyond the station is the pier where steamers leave for Portree and Stornoway. Standing on the pier one can plainly see the Isle of Skye – about four miles distant – with the rugged peaks of the Cuillin Hills standing out as clearly as if from the ocean.

There are numerous other views to be obtained from vari-

ous points of the township, which by reason of its natural position, and the efforts of the West Highland Railway, promises to develop into a thriving centre of industry in the near future.

Mallaig – 'thriving centre of industry' thanks to the West Highland line

Stations	Mileages
Fort William	
Banavie	2.5
Corpach	3.5
Locheilside	10.25
Glenfinnan	17
Lochailort	26.25
Beasdale	31
Arisaig	34.25
Morar	39
Mallaig	41.75

Mallaig station, true end of the line since the track to the pier was lifted